The Gallows, Still

Poems by Joseph Sulier

Kansas City   Spartan Press   Missouri

Spartan Press
Kansas City, Missouri
spartanpresskc.com

Copyright (c) Joseph Sulier, 2018
First Edition 1 3 5 7 9 10 8 6 4 2
ISBN: 978-1-946642-46-2
LCCN: 2018935269

Design, edits and layout: Jason Ryberg
Author photo: Raphael Maurice
Cover art: Colin Swanson-White
All rights reserved. No part of this publication may be reproduced or transmitted in any form or by any means, electronic or mechanical, including photocopying, recording or by info retrieval system, without prior written permission from the author.

Spartan Press would like to thank Prospero's Books, The Fellowship of N-finite Jest, The Prospero Institute of Disquieted P/o/e/t/i/c/s, Will Leathem, Tom Wayne, Jeanette Powers, j.d.tulloch, Jon Bidwell, Jason Preu, Mark McClane, Tony Hayden and the whole Osage Arts Community.

CONTENTS

Let fall lay rest / 1

The cycle / 2

March along / 4

The house is quiet / 5

I am the warning winds / 6

I went to see / 7

Love begets the cruelty of hope / 8

My love / 9

The wind befalls / 10

Has it never appeared perverse / 12

Lying on porcelain / 13

A nightmare of the past / 14

Should the state engage / 15

He clenched the boy's shoulder / 16

Our future / 17

You are the ape in the cage / 18

Weeping / 19

I am the butt / 20

To thrive / 22

You illuminate my door / 23

We have heard / 24

The far away whistle wail / 25

Oh faraway friends / 26

We are no rarity / 27

In a nobler age / 29

I am the real me / 30

The atmosphere is unnatural / 31
Before I am arrested by sleep / 32
I emerged from my prison / 33
The goodness of the sun / 34
There sits a globe / 35
Clutching you / 36
Crying on the dishes / 37
Enamored / 38
I am raking the leaves / 39
A cold walk in the rain / 40
A still alive / 41
If you cannot accept the human / 42
Acceptance of freedom / 43
Eat the shit / 44
I am not the bard of protest / 45
I meant to burden you / 46
You asked for blood / 47
This is my loud machine / 48
I am sitting at my window / 49
The madness of the desert / 50
My brothers groaned / 51
I feel the war subside / 52
The headlines were good today / 53
I am wretched before god / 55
I watched the caboose disappear / 56

For every perfect pearl in an otherwise putrid sea.

1.
Let fall lay rest
to ill portents
and succor e'er
the prisoner
who suffers all the whims
of idle fools

Lay me down
'neath winter snow
til sunlight shone
hath made me whole

2.
The cycle
of rejection
an effort exerted
all for naught
and you
love
inherit but
the stain of my acquaintance

(It was summer
yes
remember?
in a fragment you escape to)

The reliable rejection
is this what we are for
and nothing more?
no envy
in the brambled path
the negligible entry

(A creek behind the house
the waning moments
a few of which
were fond)

I have tarnished you
unwittingly
I have tired
of the day to day
the shame
which I relay
I will go
quietly
away

3.
March along
to the funeral song
just to say you're there
those who struggle
to forget you
yet are thriving
from your air

The gallows still
awaiting you
rest assured
your day is due

4.
The house is quiet
save for
the wheezing radiators
the softest glow of Christmas
the faintest scent of pine
the sugarplums do dance
for you
whilst I war with me and mine
no quiet
in the clamor of the mind

I wonder
how the dust collects
on covered shelves
the cat is unperplexed
by the din of the machine
we breathe the short breaths
of old men
we've seen the shit
and dodged deaths
and circled 'round the drain
like failing hair
gumming up the works
of ancient pipes

I wonder
when do we begin
to understand
the unrelenting waste
of man?

5.
I am the warning winds
which signal you seek shelter
a lesson to your children
learning well
to never speak
before they're spoken to
and even still
to form the words of someone else

I am the vendor
here to give
and never wither
from me exact
an endless tab

Come seek from me
on bended knee
the burdens
you hath never sought to bear
I will create for you
your reasons
from the air

6.
I went to see
the man on the mount
he showed me the scar
in the tree
which lightning failed to fell

The man said to me
my survival is key
that the tree
is no different
than me

7.
Love begets the cruelty of hope
it feeds us the futility of will

We are nothing
unto nothing still

8.
My love
as the abrasive unrelenting sun
yours
the softest reflection
of the forgiving moon

A metaphor to make us nauseous
do be kind
I fail at any trial
to describe

9.
The wind befalls
the trembling pine
and from the bottom up
the ashen drape of sky

I am mother's little boy
today
though we share the smoke
and speak in curses
on the porch

Oh, mother
I have seen so many things
did you know?
so much
that I could never tell you

My legs cross
like a boy
matured to man
the ember hangs
in the air
as my hand hangs
off my knee
new slippers
are the least of what we need

The wind befalls
the shedding leaves
dead and tumbling
and from the top down
the aching loss of time

10.
Has it never appeared perverse
convincing people
to pay for prisons
which they shall populate?
creating laws
from baseball calls
and dreaming
of that American apple pie
in the sky

The *criminal*
reflects the flaws
you are not able to admit
dare you not peer into their cell
lest you may find yourself within it

11.
Lying on porcelain
with a whiskey and water
watching my floating flaccid phallus
bobbing, bearded in the bubbles
vulnerable
and naked as Marat
hoping you will come to kill me
in the incensed pyre of a Pisces

12.
A nightmare of the past
ushers in
another turn around the sun
you won't be kind to anyone

13.
Should the state engage
in terroristic acts
are not all terroristic acts
permissible
by law?
for if the state does not abide
what motivations lie
for the subjects of their rule?
is it not cruel
that we should fool ourselves
selecting only power
seeking power?
that we do not trust ourselves
finds us marching towards the hour
of our willful given bondage

14.

He clenched the boy's shoulder
in reproach
and when the boy did not obey
he clenched for pain
and mother
in the background
bore a wince
and sideways glance
because she knew
what was to follow

The boy
was unswayed

15.
Our future
is the Dairy Queen
in the desert
the trailer
in purgatory

The alarm is sounding
your shift is up

16.
You are the ape in the cage
subdued to observe
resigned and sedate

You are the subject
to the crowd
the object
to perturb

You are the prisoner
to uphold
the example
to forget
the panther pacing round
the madness of consequence

Never seek
to plead your truth
give silent death
remain aloof

The only lesson learned
is not to fail
and never speak

17.
Weeping
when a stranger overhears
that you're from different parts
and offers you
the stub of his blunt

Weeping
when two men in the park
bring to you their brightness

Weeping
at a queer
confessional

There is northern
in their south
there are rebel
statues

Weeping
at the contradictions

18.
I am the butt
stamped out in the gutter
longing to be above you
with my love
to fuel the sun
far beyond
its due destruction
the wind
which animates the trees
instead of just
the scratched up knees

I have desires too
you know
I am more
than just the punchline
of your cruel pathetic show
I will beam bright
below you
I will be more
than nothing more

My love
she leaves me notes
when I'm so low
to let me know
we'll go

beyond the scraps
which we're expected to survive on

Some somber morning
I'll awake
to see the star again
above
and I shall join it
in its flame
(it's just a claim)

19.
To thrive
in the harsh glare
of sobriety
to face yourself
as flawed
to defy
the pull of pride
to resist
the false empowerment
of vanity

A meditation
for moving on
an intent
to evolve

Let go
and leave revenge to rot

20.
You illuminate my door
when no one dares to enter
I am humbled
in your virtues of forgiveness
and am brightest in your shadow

You've filled our rooms
with herbs and blooms
and suffered
'neath the cruelty of man
the knowing natured scorn
of idle man
you are
your mother's cherished daughter
I am
no mother's rightful son

I have known
so many women nurtured well
it was you who led me
errant out of hell

21.
We have heard
the serpent's whisper
and sought knowledge
of forbidden fruit
and naked
we are shunned from goodness

Let he
who is without sin
be the bully to believe

22.
The far away whistle wail
at the window
and the rumbling of the rails
sings you off
into intoxicated slumber
and you wonder
if awaking makes a difference
if a remainder in dreams
would repel the reality
of another pained morning
wincing at the sun

23.
Oh faraway friends
I do grieve
'neath the pall
of power
hear you now
my weakness
in futility

The dogs inherit
no great revolving orb
no life is truly lived
through fear

We defer
the wisdom of subtlety
to absolutes
we seek to win a race
which has no goal

Oh faraway friends
hear you now
my weakness
in the fight
I fear we wage
for naught

24.
We are no rarity
my thoughts and I
on the precipice
of nothing

It was winter once
I recall
and again it was
every year to follow

I was young
when I watched the bird egg
break
and wept
because the universe
did not weep
the children thought it soft
so I wept alone

The caps melt
and it means nothing
the power remains
and means nothing
the something we assign
is drifting river wood

Every perfect patterned snowflake
melts away
and is forgot
the pebbles skip the surface
the ripples dissipate

25.

In a nobler age
I'd have been a soldier
a muscle in whole
for the use of idea men
I would carry out
the solemn duty of death
with no objection

Now
if I must embrace
the part of pariah
if I must suffer violence
in exchange for redemption
if I must burden my body
and bleed
to break you of your bondage
it is my duty, I decree
as a soldier of the free

26.
I am the real me
on the page
and not the cruel caricature of youth
you leave in your wake
though I am weak
when you're away
and ever prideful
of my lover

I've heard it said
behind every mediocre man
lies the power
of a surer anchored woman

27.
The atmosphere is unnatural
the smooth
all creased and rigid
the sky is opened up
the inevitable return

I do not know
that I am good
I only know
that I've considered

28.
Before I am arrested by sleep
I watch your shoulder glow
in the soft light of the Christmas tree
awakened by your kiss
which curls me up into the covers
like the touched antennae of a slug

Carly said I was a good boy
and I believe her
others said that I was bad
and I believe them too
I need not wrestle
with a tarnished reputation
for I need not deny
the worst of my humanity
it keeps me humble
in my furtive cell

Sometimes when I'm alone
I scream
for lack of other release
and the new year
means nothing new to me
just a dog-eared page of history
I resolve to need no editor
It's the mistakes which help me see

29.
I emerged from my prison
into the brilliant blue of sky
though just as the sky
is but an illusion of light
so too was my freedom
an illusion of flight

I rode
on my own
down the road
through the sun
and down to the river
bloated with debris
the river lay claim
to the remnants of trees

I looked for you
but found only space
and recalled
all the shock on your face

30.
The goodness of the sun
is not enough
the grass will all go brown
the softest wisp of smoke
was lifted to the sky
the night they laid you down

31.
There sits a globe
atop my desk
and thus I spin it
just to know
there is a hand
outstretched to mine
which shall never know a friend
two eyes
which struggle in the dark
just to find the faintest spark

32.
Clutching you
for warmth and comfort
in the cold terror
of my nightmare bed

The seasonal observation
of the ebb and flow
of the note

The timely preparation
of the bird
the waning appeal
of the leftovers

Adorning the corpse
of a tree
and wondering
why I feel it suffer

Should auld acquaintance
be forgot
and never brought to mind?
I'll be fine

33.
Crying on the dishes
and contemplating death
you wonder to yourself
if this is what they meant
when they told you
your dreams will come true

You must accept
that just to fight
is not to win
you will be felled again

34.
Enamored
by the music of old men
because I wonder
when I will be there
when
can I leave it all behind?
engulfed
in the chasm of memory

Fuck you
to the folly of youth
I will be old
and left alone
I will forget
the bitter spurn
of listless adolescence
and remember myself
anew

35.
I am raking the leaves
please
leave me be
and the most elegant blooms
shall burst forth
from me
and I
into eternity

36.
A cold walk in the rain
past the apartment room
consecrated with our leery laden love
past the fallen flowers
of the summer
to the beat
of a drummer with no band

37.
A still alive
still life
a dinner table
rife
with relatives
healing stones
a fallen soldier
the painted world
of old

There is a rabbit's severed head
I am certain he is dead

38.
If you cannot accept the human
as it is
the conscious conflicted creature
borne up
from the depths of its detriments
separate in nature
as unfortunately aware
how then
to cope with your own corruption?

We forge ahead
from our faults
ever forward
rather than to profit
from our perfection
ever prideful

39.
Acceptance of freedom
is not simply
acceptance of goodness
of joy
it is
as well
acceptance of violence
disorder
the folly of control

Men grow content
in their prisons
because they grow well nourished
and nourishment
sees man grow plump with comfort
and the indifferent bliss
of ignorance
they forget
the richness of tragedy
the wholeness of pain
the experience
not always agreeable

I teach this to myself
to remember
and share it with you
to be sure

40.
Eat the shit
of intellectuals
and grin through soiled teeth
submit your worth
to trail the pack
who buy what they lack
and you let them for cheap
they're just riding the wave
that you crave
you'll find nothing of you
you can save

41.
I am not the bard of protest
nor the bard of party lines
I am the bard imprisoned
the leaf
despised by trees
the feral spirit
no one frees

My errors
unforgiven
my atonement unto you
I shall make do
and prove it true

42.

I meant to burden you
with such a lengthy elocution
a detailed log of life
of all the hours, minutes, days
creating wholeness in a man
but all that I reflect
is yet an errant missive
the man still scattered
incomplete
seldom hale
a goal we scarcely ever reach

43.
You asked for blood
and I have bled
you have asked for silence
and I cease to speak
you have asked repentance
and I oblige
you ask for isolation
and I do disappear

What now, do you ask?
shall I descend the void?
shall I cede the keys
to the prison of my Elba?
would you ask
that I survive on moonlight?
is my great offense
an aberration in man?
what relation in my nature
will you grant within your own?
are we not all
rejected from the womb
afraid
and prone to error?

I've accepted purgatory
though I'm unconvinced
of heaven's ensuing embrace

44.
This is my loud machine
for when I'm feeling quiet
this is the bolder me
for when I'm feeling frightened
I take a sip
and pour on out
about
just anything at all
like the roach in the ashtray
smells like dad
or any other thought
I might have had

This is where I like to be
when I'm allowed
much preferred
to saying it aloud
I'm talking to myself again
or god
or you
it's the one thing I can do

45.
I am sitting at my window
waiting for the snow

The clouds have called the country
to be blanketed in white
so the blood is easier to find

46.
The madness of the desert
the many facets of the inferno
we drove
with the many grasping demons
in our wake
tell me of the flowers
that we pick
and I'll ensure these mighty roads
we labor through
ornament our steed
with the bones of burdened beasts

I'm assured that you're awaiting me
when I'm weeping on my own

47.
My brothers groaned
at the passing procession
of a funeral
I met the mourner's gaze
in a stoned and solemn haze

The Great One
skating bloated in Busch Stadium
the dream team line
of warm remembered feats
we're all looking back
nostalgic
hold on a little tighter
as it slips

No longer seasonal
nor annual
we count the seconds
not the days

48.
I feel the war subside
as my love is painting pictures
exorcising imperfections
we're astride
into the sun
I am melting
in her mercy

So long I learned
to not expect
no room for the weak
no love for the lost
to stumble adrift
an errant path unlit

Now you
with no conditions
how shocked am I
to be myself

49.
The headlines were good today
a golden harp played softly
over Syria
the dead are rising up
among the graves
the new leaders of men
have given up their warring ways
and halted warming of the world
the guns have given way
to greater things
and plastic washed away
from waterways
it is a new great age
we build
our votes will see
the cabinets filled
with the hippies of yesteryear
do not fear
there is no more black and white
for every man is grey
it is a brilliant hopeful day

Jesus throws hail marys
for the Patriots
on Sundays
did I awake to something new?
hallowed Hillary has won

decreed the law as fun
rejoices everyone

I dreamt I was a fish
I drowned

50.
I am wretched before god
repulsive in the mirror
as a fallen child
ignored by grace

I have burnt
below the sun
I have cowered in my dwelling
yet you come to me
imparting your regards

I've defied
an offered hand
of your compassion
I am loathe to pass your door

Success is but awaking
and dreams are far from pure
my sleep is neither respite
nor redemption
my new day begs
to lay me down once more

51.
I watched the caboose disappear
along the waterway
the frozen flailing flag
emblazoned on the side
the sky was grey and misty-eyed
I closed my coat against the chill
with Christmas almost here

Goodbye

Joseph Sulier was born and raised in the simple poverty of Fenton Missouri and currently resides in the city of St. Louis. Sulier has been published in several literary journals including *52nd City, The U. City Review, The Curator Magazine* and *RINE* and has had several collections of poetry published including *The Ruins of a Rube* (Permanent Sleep Press), *A House Full of Broken Instruments* (Permanent Sleep Press), *The Dogs Are Winning* (Calico Grounds Press), *Only Death is Certain* (Get Born Press) and *Never Well Again* (Get Born Press).

This project was made possible, in part, by generous support from the Osage Arts Community.

Osage Arts Community provides temporary time, space and support for the creation of new artistic works in a retreat format, serving creative people of all kinds — visual artists, composers, poets, fiction and nonfiction writers. Located on a 152-acre farm in an isolated rural mountainside setting in Central Missouri and bordered by ¾ of a mile of the Gasconade River, OAC provides residencies to those working alone, as well as welcoming collaborative teams, offering living space and workspace in a country environment to emerging and mid-career artists. For more information, visit us at www.oac.com

www.ingramcontent.com/pod-product-compliance
Lightning Source LLC
Chambersburg PA
CBHW021450080526
44588CB00009B/785